The Wind Speaks

The Wind Speaks

Poems

Elsa Johnson

GREEN WRITERS PRESS | *Brattleboro, Vermont*

Printed in the United States

10 9 8 7 6 5 4 3 2 1

Green Writers Press is a Vermont-based publisher whose mission is to spread a message of hope and renewal through the words and images we publish. Throughout we will adhere to our commitment to preserving and protecting the natural resources of the earth. To that end, a percentage of our proceeds will be donated to environmental activist groups. Green Writers Press gratefully acknowledges support from individual donors, friends, and readers to help support the environment and our publishing initiative.

Giving Voice to Writers & Artists Who Will Make the World a Better Place

Green Writers Press | Brattleboro, Vermont
www.greenwriterspress.com

ISBN: 978-1-9505849-5-6

THE PAPER USED IN THIS PUBLICATION IS PRODUCED BY MILLS COMMITTED
TO RESPONSIBLE AND SUSTAINABLE FORESTRY PRACTICES.

oh   my   beloved   my touch
will be   as breathing
leaves   and blossoms

fling wide your doors

CONTENTS

Testimony

I will speak now with other voices   :   quick-silver
chipmunk   offering the sunflowers   for
one more day's safe grace   :   whippoorwill   legend --
saver of lost souls   haunting the wood's edge --
calling the dusk moths home   :   hawk   gifter of
quick death   she of the silent   swift-moving
shadow   and ice cold heart   :   vulture   gleaner
wing-rider   wind-soarer   he of the priesthood
of death   :   hummingbird   chittering   at top
of linear locust trees   :   and the wood drake
resting on water   I will speak with
the great heron   the night heron   the 'fisher'
flashing   low over the lake   and with
the deer   browsing at stream's edge   without fear

And I will speak   with those that speak   in stranger
tongues   the small ring-necked snake   writhing
loosened from her sheltering rock   the strong
jawed turtle   lurking   under the water:
Yellow-jackets   that sting   and chase   to sting
again   :   the devouring mantis   --   and
the delicate damselflies   she sometimes
hunts   I will speak with   bees   butterflies   dazed
in the milkweed   with goldenrod   --   all that
multitude of   tiny insects   buzzing   :
purple   pungent   oregano   yellow
eyed blue buddleia   crystal crusted day
lilies   and bee-glad phlox   I will speak with
star-burst   syllables   of cimicifuga
of red crocosmia   drunkenly sprawling

I will learn   to speak   with the lichen
In the speech of   grey-green filigree   covering
branches   coating stone   biding time   --   I will
learn   and speak   in the soft green voice of moss
that covers the feet   of the ancient oaks
dying now   riddled by borer   riven
with wilt   I will learn   these tunneled codes   and
speak with worms   with mold   with microscopic
mycorrhizal fungi   leaf mulch   with dark
decay   --   the deep secret language of
the mysterious   complexity of
dirt   duff   ruffled rhubarb   and all that
erotic   unfurling   of spring   new risen
out of   the luminous dying   of fall

First Snow

We woke   to find   Hakuro Nishiki --
small Japanese willow   leaves still attached   --
burdened with first snow   It is a shrub grafted to
stout trunk   that hummingbirds used   to keep eye
on nectar jars   we hung from eaves   Summer lengthened
the supple branches   increasing undulation
by slight swells of air   The birds held tight to billows
as the fronds surged   This was their watch-out
tower   where they enforced   air-control-by-willow
For us   it was like looking down through water
to where   sea anemones waved below   This snow
wet and   heavy   drags our ocean down to
motionless   I should have pruned these branches
weeks ago   but couldn't bear to shear the sea

In Memoriam

In remembrance of Kathy Jaye

What I remember is the child   –   slender
long-limbed   Viking blond   –   sitting on her horse
in sunshine   :   calm   balanced   unflappable   --
although   surely   there must have been moments
of childish tears   Years passed   When next I saw
her   I learned   she rode a darker horse
unwilling   and too soon   toward an unknown
place   she did not want to go   She was as
before   --   slender   long-limbed   Viking blond
Although   surely   there must have been tears
at the hard hand dealt her   she rode as a
warrior bred   :   calm   balanced   unflappable
She rode with a laugh   --   rode forward in
sunshine   with a smile   like a spear in the hand

At Twenty Two

I wrote   that frost had tipped   my tree-branched heart
and   --   as though in a moment of profound
truth   --   I wrote   'Everything is shred of its
frivolity'   In yet another poem
then   I wrote   :   'amabo   *I shall love'*
because the path   forward   seemed so remote
 it needed to be met with   defiance
Obscured   I lost my way   which is not to
say   that all that has passed between   was not
worth doing   some of it unchosen   and yet
I've learned the path also   finds you   and even
if you choose wisely   it   blunders   you
to pain   --   and joy   What did I know of love ?
I was so green   so green   --   there was no frost

Before Electricity

Our friend in Iceland   sent the scene   :   a grave
yard   stone-cross studded   grey-sky-grey-sea   and
in another shot   a rainbow   muted   --
melting   :   pale cold sun   a-slant old stone walls
It   is always changing   he says   That was
on the Solstice   --   two hours and fourteen minutes
of diluted daylight   My mind   boggles
over this   :   twenty-one hours and six
minutes of dark winter night   night after
night   --   all of them   tunnel hours   Our northern
sires knew nothing else   Perhaps it was a gift
that slow time   to sing   to carve   to dream
and love   in darkness   No - no turning back
not for us   we are through that looking glass

COUNTING   DAYS – NIGHTS -- YEARS

Night comes early   this time of year   Short twilight
days   fade to dull washed over dim   northeast
Ohio winter days   edged to collapse --
dark   into deeper darkness   Entire days of
not-day-not-night   almost-but-not-quite   gloaming
Solstice   in a few short days   Not a good
climate for   New Grange effect   The sun
so rarely shines   one would not think to build
a long   cold   slot of stone   for sun to creep
up   and back down   again   One might wait years --
How many   millennium   would it take
to connect   cause and effect   in this climate?
Brighter gloaming on snow-glow nights   Brighter
nights than days   when snow is grounded

MOONSTUCK

It feels long as a season   these dark hours of
night   --   these dry hours   when sleep almost enters
the room but then   both eager and afraid
trembling   pulled by   anticipation's   tide
dithers in the door   Sleep's pulled by the moon
this way   then that   Restless   the moon's power
stirs the sap of all women   waxing in
our tidal blood   that men don't share   Even
as we grow white   and dry   it holds sway   --   enthralls
strengthens   Awake at midnight   we read :
at two   eat cheese   with crackers   :   at four   think
there is a poem in this   *somewhere*   Tomorrow
we sisterhood of blood will say   It was
a full moon   *a night season*   We couldn't sleep

MEDITATION AT THE WINTER SOLSTICE

When I was young   I stacked my skis outside my
door   strapped them on   on winter nights   floated
almost   soundless   past blackened woods   and fields
gleaming   bright   in darkness   (hint of borealis
in blue-black sky)   But these days   creep   to Solstice --
to beyond   when   we begin to look for --
notice   hope   for the almost imperceptible
lengthening   of curtailed light   toward larger
hours   The bulk of winter looms ahead   cold
and beautiful   but someone has to shovel
walk   and drive   --   at this age one feels   once   is
enough   :   lake effect weather   dark   to aging
bones   that wish to strap on skis   and flee   fear-
less   into wild and quiet   snow-stunned   nights

Remnant Anomaly

It pauses me   this *thing*   I have found   that
is not of   this wakening world   hidden
halfway up the slope   halfway   up the trail   in
winter's windfall of   downed limbs   dead leaves   last
year's dry crushed grass   :   Stiff leather   with battered
bits / tufts / and on it   patchy-fur   --   a tired *thing*
lying   lasting here   Some creature's coat
The winter's   beasts of prey   have done their work
well   This is not the first   part   I've found
Decay   has long since   eroded out   its
essence   --   spirit of what lived   :   its run   its
grace   bound   bounce   --   all fled   Toeing it over
do I not touch   briefly   the fear   the breath
/   the short chase   /   the tear   /   the taking down

THE GREEN KNIGHT

Look   --   here are the marks of hooves   and a spot
of blood on the packed snow   He's come   It is
that coldest time   before the tide of spring
sweeps in   --   time of the green night   that swells
the buds   of the redbud tree   the shadblow
and the maple   In the backyard   late last
fall   I cut spent heads   off hydrangeas   --
they stood all winter   in this   amputated   state
Yesterday   I saw in passing   below their
truncated stems   swollen buds   :   that green
devil   pushing   that thick fluid through the tube
Morning   --   pale moon gone from the platinum
sky   the birds erupt in pagan chorus
There is no   *no*   that force knows

How the Orgy Begins

Honeyberry leafed out   last night   Her pale
tight   tiny   flower buds   are straining   *Wait - wait*
the birds cry !   *there are no bees to pollinate*
you yet!   The first grey-green leaves of buddleia
uncurl   Poking   amid half-digested
leaf mold   finds   fragile carcass of insect --
possibly bumblebee   --   and over there   one
scant handful   of   ultra   violet   irises --
while here   lurid   in its red   unfurling
almost   obscene   rhubarb   :   like a bright
vulva   aroused from dirt   Last year's debris
shouts   *take me!*   *away!*   while this year's new life
claws   out of the ground   and spring's sparrows call :
where? / there?   *Is it time?*   *who? / now? / quick! / quick!*

Prune -- a Story

In the spring orchard   /   plum trees bloom   /   petals fall on a poet's
shoulders   /   like shorn fleece from sheep   /   fruit sets   /   a shepherd
shepherds the herd   /   to the meadows   /   to the high sky

Plum   :   the fruit of a small tree   usually
eaten out of hand   when ripe   or   when dried
called prune and stored / stowed   shepherd's sustenance
Prune   :   a black whole   a dark sun   a plum   flesh
etched   reduced   wrinkled   a desert flower   sharp
fresh tongue of the sun   concentrated   soothed
Prune   :   a removal   an action taken
To cut clean   place your blade   where the branch
arches away from trunk   to minimize the wound
If the blade is sharp   the limb falls away
Prune   :   edit   --   a poet's work   Cut the plum(b)
lines   the tethers   Fell the fruit   Bruise the limbs
Prune the page   The words   wounded   trail across
paper like   red   plasmic connections

Prune : an alteration   if you wrap   twine
around your fingers   don't be surprised if
when the sheep   bolts   the tips shear   away
Shear :   cutting off   The sheep   down from the hill
mill in confusion   they tythe   they protest
Tythe :   tax   the master's share   usually given
in/voluntarily   the rich man takes
the pick of the plums   the best of the fleece
Fleece :   acquire through chicanery   The shepherd's
fleeced / the sheep de-fleeced   Their thick pelts plumbed
Plumb : to dig deep / worm taxes : holes in black wholes
subterranean   chicaneries of
plums :   soft drupes   warm from sun   The poor poet
sits under the trees   S/he prunes   S/he plum(b)s

Late in the day   the fleeced sheep sleep   the shorn shepherd sits
under the sheared trees   under the warm sun
the poet plum{b{s   the plums prune   the sky is high

17

GREEN FUSION

We're   not really in control here   I realize
stepping   out my back door   this May morning
and there   assaulted   by spring's green bore   that
tide-like   overrules   my plans and inclinations   --
Sensations of attack   the trees green leaves
burn neon   --   a visible vibration   –   and
where backyard grass grows   inch an hour   a buckeye
sprouted overnight   Meanwhile   honeysuckle
sends out tendriled shoots   :   wends tight to the ground
War   :   irresistible   --   *Green Peace* a misnomer
pitiful   our arrogance   as this great wave
builds a sea   Only with great effort   do we
maintain primacy   Sovereigns of the world
we think ourselves   :   nature   a biddable   she

SNIP

is how I know   the god   has found me --
the blood god   This time   just a tiny snip
from the fourth finger   from which   years ago
he ripped off the tip   I found it   had it
sewn back on   In an eye blink   that's how fast
he strikes   when your head is turned away   your
mind on task   but   not on the steel blades that
cuts through tough   resistant   plant stems   like soft
buttery flesh   *Snip* .   We are profligate
with blood   our species   --   begin small   :   a boy's
foreskin   a tiny (finger)tip   but it
grows in us   at last   --   the blood god   :   lusting --
needing   driving   some poor souls   blood bath mad   :
I am so   weary   of blood sacrifice

It's Everything

I'm picking   serviceberries   to the sound
of seethe   that sea sound   of the wind   high
in the rigging   of the trees   hundreds of
miles from ocean   reminding me   again
how   without water   life could not exist
on this planet   The sea flows through us all
even though we are far away   --   through our
salted blood   through the birds' blood   (with whom we
share these berries)   even through the trees   There
are unsalted seas   closer home   choppy
and dangerous   that   --   though good to see   to
hear   --   do not stir the seethe in me   I am
picking berries   to the sound of sea   :   three
for the birds   --   two for me   ---   and one for thee

The Peninsula

for Seamus Heaney

Sometimes   when you have nothing to say   it
is because   water and ground   swallowed
the words   They're in the dark   and will never
arrive   The Sky Road's like that   --   the road round
the peninsula   rides   toward a drunken
sea and sky   There is no horizon   :   sky
and the glazed sea meld   The white washed gabled
cottage   that you mentioned   is at the point
-- a compass for swallowed words   It is as you
said :   the sea   the islands   riding the sea
the road   riding the grassed hill   and the ground rising
Sometimes   when you have nothing to say   after
a long drive   it is because water   and
ground in extremity   have swallowed worlds

When Fondness Fails

She loves this word   deliquesce (nce)   It is
a word that   rolls   then slides   round the echo
chamber of the mouth bell   The mouth hears and
the ears   tell   a sustained syllabescence
Deliquescence   demonstrates   the under
enduring bond   She salts him   and the bond
dissolves   --   an unhappy   de – composition
It is a heart - rose rupture   --   The petals
of love   made dissolute   fall off one by
one   What remains is   essence   (which is no
ease   for her heart's discomfort)   :   attar of
Gabrielle   delicate reminder of
her heart's heat   scent of anger   an odor of
unhappiness   --   brave deliquescence

Poppies

Conjure   a poem   out of air   about
love   --   not the flimsy idle-fancy sort   but
love of the deep kind   the kind deep love
that takes root   in the soil   of the heart   and
anchors there   so that when storms blow   as blow
they must for life's mortality   that tether
strains but holds   Conjure poems : not love
No wispy thing can last   --   the part for show
must come and go   Those fragile blooms   of orange
flower glow   so tissue fine   that leap   our
hearts   toward thrill   all fail   and fall apart at
the least touch   or wind   Love is the part you
don't see : heart root   tapped straight down into
where the rich red   sustaining   rills   flow

SEETHE

Not susurration   this present wind   --   that would
be a softer stirring   the trees' leaves tendering
whispers of intimate   rubbings   *touch*   green leaf
to green leaf   in quiet   communication
But this wind is a boil   a seethe of leaves   whipped
funneled to furious   yet not destructive   --   a life-
full sound   and so   sustaining   Eyes closed
this seethe could be   the sound of a strong   tide
running   on a blind night   sea   swirled   and churned
to froth and foam   spume and fume   also wind
driven   The moment ?   Immersive :   sight nothing
sound everything   Solace   :   when time stops
(or seems to)   --   eyes closed   ears open   hear
this roaring sibilance   born   not   of rage

The first   transcendence   is a reaching out   as chest
expands   to create *pull*   for the first breath   drawing
all that is *other*   inwards   a bellows   sparking
marriage : air -- fueling flesh   Our beginnings --
like this -- depend on words   and on the worlds of
others : immanence and exhalation   similar   for tree
and fig   and the black-cap chickadee   and us   We
know   the tree breathes   silent   and unseen   and
the fig's nipple   begins   at the throat swell
where the bee pillaged pollen   and   sweetness
entered   and was stored   Desire : as in the bright eyes
of the black-cap chickadees   whose small breasts --
lifting -- take inward clean bare breaths   and
Sudden!   Songs of the world fling   outward

BLUE FLAGS

We stop   to gather   full pods   from the milkweed
plants   where they grow   in the meadow   amid
tall grasses   and golden rod   that waves
as the wind blows   as the rain falls   and runnels
the ground   toward the swale   where we planted blue
flags one spring   in the water   and sunflowers
beside   --   The milkweed pods are like fat fish
which we pull from their stalks   and carry
in our shirt pockets   our pants pockets   and
in our wet arms   to the run-off ditch   where our
hands grow   sticky   with white sap   as we pull
apart pods for the seeds inside   silvered   --
lined up like   fish scales   tied to silk threads   which
rend   and scatter   and drift   in wet air

THEN THERE IS LONGING

You cannot *plan* to go there   It comes to you
as   when once   a leaf   that by gravity's
law   should fall   spun suspended   --   and once when
death dazzled eyes saw lilies   so minutely
each   shimmered petal's atoms   effervesced
The world   collapsing   funnels   into your
brain   like a black bore   born there   is pulling
you in   till you are one   Or it
can be an   opening   unexpected
a latch   sprung   on the lid of the head   so
brain exhales the motes of   *me*   out   and
a million   *me* - threads   expand to breathing
nothing   that is wholeness   that feels like
home   :   then it is done

A Song of Gentle Extirpation

Some plants   that you invite   to your garden
can never over-stay 'welcome'   even
when they overstep   Sea oats aren't like that :
They spread / take up space/ crowd / sprawl like their name
sprawls on a page   and   given a year or
two   they inundate   drown out phlox   lilies
agastache   --   the plants we love   that beacon
butterflies   and all kinds of bees   Our eyes
need space   to pause   to rest   to breathe   Air
that seems to hold   nothing   holds our eyes   --   which
land   dry off their wings   then fly on again
This grass   that works to bind beach dunes   stilling
sand against the surge   works wrongly   in my garden
graceful though it be   when soft winds   stir

(Wild) Life in the Inner Suburbs

Walking to my car   parked in the street   I find
them   --   studies in dun   Looking like big dun   dogs
Looking like   someone opened the closet door   --
found moths   in all the good dun suits   the no
color suits   of shadow   Looking patched up and
lean   with long dun bodies   a-top legs like   twigs   :
Gazing at me with   soft brown eyes   a bit   anxious
like   there's a name on the tip of their tongues
--   if they could only   remember   everything
would be all right   --   like they think   I'm thinking
there goes the neighborhood   when all I'm really
thinking   is   up to now you haven't eaten
my daylilies   Dammit   :   Don't start now

July...

...in the summer garden   :   The plants that seemed
in May so fresh   --   like young girls standing discrete
in pristine green uniforms   of promise   now
throw off all restraint   No more apartness
they declare   No space between   They twine   and
drape   and lean   against each other   giddy --
display their petticoat parts   Each night   daylilies
paint new bright faces   while among them   thin
crocosmia sprawls   her many arms round all
red mouths open   for bees   for birds   --   oh
delirious fecundity   and fertile chaos !
But see there   that sturdy   sunflower   fellow
that quietly   parts   the flash girls   as he grows tall?
he belongs to August   September   the coming fall

High Summer

It is not the sound of cicadas   but that
other sound   drone   that   hummm
mmm   as of the energy of many   bees   at work
in an unseen hive   almost resonance   almost
vibration   almost   palpable   as it seeps through
the pores   into every living   and non-living
core   In the thick heat   the red daylilies   turn
greasy   the sunflowers wilt   and yet-to-bloom
phlox   and actea   weigh down   from sound   Dirt
cracks   Dry meadow grasses   tassle   to seed
Milkweed   turns   blossom to pod   One blood red
leaf   from a black gum tree   falls   to ground
Overnight   some peak   it seems   has come   then
gone   --   even as it arrived   it's leaving

The Turn

After my work-crew teens went home   I stayed at
the bridge   indulging   my perfectionist tendencies
scraping   the last of the moss   and woody weeds
from the stone's joints   and so   discovered   tucked
within a crack   a tiny   ring-neck snake   pencil slim
perfect   in its neat grey skin   Minutes later   riled
yellow-jackets   swarmed from a hole   --   stinging through
my gloves   my clothes   and chased me from the bridge
They could not   be allowed to live   where people pass   so
close each day   but later   I thought   --   is the wasp less
perfect   than the snake?   Are not   all   nature's children
innocents   living   obedient to their calling?   Each day
begins without fanfare   is engaged   unsuspecting   not
knowing   when the turn will come   --   if there will be one

Vulture on the World Tree

It was   new territory   to us   We rode
the air currents   to get there   up-drafts
We spread our wings out   wide   the tips tilted
up   the wind riffling   through them   There were three
of us   circling   We smelled dead things   We eat
dead things   The scent of dead things travels   When
we catch   that   smell   we will fly a long way
A meal should be dead   but not ripe   :   You need
presence in the land of the dead   You need a
tree   that stands alone   You need to see what else
is out there in that land   We can clear a corpse
in a couple hours   --   thorough   --   we don't notice
what it is   If you have a dead thing
to get rid of   you can do worse than us

To a Spider

It was a strange place to call   home   If you'd been
bigger   you'd not have fit that gap   in the passenger
side mirror   where you'd anchored one end of your
filigree web   I'd glance over   as I sped down
the road   and there you'd be   not tucked safe in your
den   but gale tossed   scrunched to a blip   a small
ship   clutching threads   When I'd arrive   where I
was going   thinking to find you   desiccated   –
dead   –   you'd unfurl your spider legs   no worse
for wear   I began to think you liked it   You
went everywhere with me   until the day I
chose for you a   less dangerous life   (I hoped)
Miss you!   See you still   :   goggles   jacket
thin silk scarves   trailing   in the slip-stream wind

Be Here Now

What else   would one write   on a fairest day?
Yesterday   overhead   the clouds flew by   like
fluffed white dragons   strung out   horizontally
battalions   no – legions !   lined up against
perfect blue   Today's heavens have changed three
times this last hour   --   wisps first   tattered   as if
breath ripped apart in some great battle   --   then
infinite   pale   and   totally   cloudless   sky
Now?   Dragon spawn   Today's all sea rush   --
a constant in-rushing   wall   :   sound   --   wave
upon wave   --   wearing away   relentless and
without emotion   Thus   what else can I say   but
Great Spirit   Dragon Breath   oh   cloud and air
let me be *present*   *Here*   :   Let me be   *now*

LISTENING TO CLOUDS

Breaking clouds   the weather forecast said   and
so I wondered   what clouds sound like   when they
break   Surely the cirrus clouds   faint feathers and
threads   high up   in the atmosphere   sound of
harp strings   and distant crystal bells   struck
just before   shatter   sweet brief hints of
music   gone   and cumulonimbus clouds   --
giant cream accumulations   are   white walls
or   blooms   that have grown heavy --   sound of   booms
bassoons   and cymbals   struck   as drama peaks
and rain descends   While stratus clouds --   flattened
dark   and bruised   like flesh   thick   grey   and
brooding   --   sound of   lamentation   flung
low to the ground   that muffles break

Epistemology of Loss

I went out this morn   to thank   the daylilies
whose time is passing   I'm grateful for their
lives   now spent   The old blossoms shrivel   shrink
then fall   I used to -- but no longer --   tidy
up   Let what comes from dirt   return to dirt
It happens   at every scale   :   dirt   flower
tree   we   me   thee   the planet   galaxy
the universe   That   is where my mind goes
as the lily fails   while the white   glorious
sweet scented phlox comes on   Who can mourn one
bloom   in such circumstance?   They say   God is in
the details   but   neglect to say which ones
Dirt / or bud ?   Fade / or flower ?   always those
annoying questions   How?   Who?   Why?   and so on

In Connecticut

Above the beach   at Hammonasset   a whirl of
many swallows circled   just below where clouds
formed   flat-bottomed   as though resting on
a surface we could not see   --   piling up   --
billowing   above   into the hued sky   Just there
was where the swallows   flew their continuous
rotation   The water was New England cold
We lingered only an hour   When we left
the swallows still   winged   and swirled   sustained
by   what ?   --   we could not see   Early evening
on my son's front porch   we watched two quarrel
some hummingbirds visit a feeder   High   high
above   a clearly modeled   three dimensional moon
hung   waxing   in a still bright sky

Sunset Song

I   too   have woken   in the dead of night
to the flicker of light   and the muted
booms   of a nearing storm   and thrown on my
shoes   to flee   into the blackness   along
the muddy lane   brushing the hot wires
twice   racing the storm   to the far pasture
where the shod horses graze   in the unsafe
night   to bring them back home   to safety
They bolt at the first strikes   --   the horses   --   plunge
and   fly   down the narrow track   by wind and
noise whipped on   by the crackling   the crashing
above   and the fierce hard lash   of the fast rain
For who can outrun the storm?   now   or ever   --
The deluge comes   passes   comes again

THOUGHTS WHILE PETTING THE CAT

The facts of life   are not what you think   they are   –
the vulgar drive of sex   that demanding need
of body   --   the explanation inexorably
biological   the exquisite sensitivity
of nerve ends flaring up   at touch   like small
galaxies   to life   No   it is that other force
equally embodied   the source   vaguer
The inexplicable mystery   of fog   how it
seeks its ways   and favorites   --   not always deserved
Veers toward one flower   color   face   book   song   place
landscape   country   god   How the heart stumbles   at
grace   the way one person moves through space   or
this small cat that   trusting   purrs before strokes
No   no   love is nebula   therefore   --   be kind

DEMON LOVER

When my demon lover   comes to bed   he drapes
his black furred body   across the pillow   above
my head   He has issues around intimacy   No
matter how hard he tries   he   cannot   get   close
enough   pushes   his head   into   my head   o
ver   and over   trying to make of us   one head
one breath   while I gently   push him away   over
and over   until -- exasperation!   I pitch his
body   down   to the far end of the bed   Ah -- sweet
sleep   Hours later   my husband wakes to find   my
demon lover between us   hunkered down   on my
right shoulder   Head tucked close to my neck
foreleg stretched across my chest   as if to say :
Possession   --   nine tenths of the law   She's mine

This Old House

One hundred years old   almost   my house that
I live in   is a map   of half done things :
garden growth   erupting   off one side   tough
dandelion punctured grass   on the other
Front porch   littered   with summer's tools   winter's
salts   and shovels   The kitchen has needed
a makeover   since before we bought it
(twenty plus years   now)   and the bathroom floor's
tiny white octagonal tiles   are cracked
width-wise   :   (some critical system is sinking
basement-ward   toward hell)   But   each numbered day
lies   open   to the warmth   of the south sun
and   though apart   living and dining room
flow together   in good marriage

Structural Correction

In my pocket I keep   rebar   Of course   it
doesn't fit   It grows   or shrinks   of its own whim –
parts of it   hang out   and drag behind me
clank   clank   I have no use for it   and there
is always more   a burden ever with me
When I go to bed   and put my night clothes
on   I find rebar there   and my day clothes
empty   It's hard to sleep with rebar   You
feel you've spent the night   with hard straight lies   Don't
have pockets in your clothes   you say   I've tried :
First   there's nothing   but soon   a pucker grows
Then there's a pocket   with rebar in it
Something   is trying   to reinforce   my
vertebrae   with steel   It just gets   displaced

To My Shadow

Oh my shadow   most nebulous love   what
will you do   when I die   --   as someday
I must   You   who are tethered to me   will you
be torn away   faithful follower   be
left   and lost   wandering untied   --   ether
seeking one small   current   amid an
invisible tide   What will my shade   do
when I am gone to dirt   or pyre ?   As I
am in love with the world   and all
its beauty   does   he   love it too?   When I am
reduced to atom   and he to mote   will
he know me?   Will I seek him in the worm's
close home?   Will he seek me in the wind ?   --   in
the crystal   crusted   on the flower's rim

"You have it   wrong"   s/he said   stretching back on
the chaise lounge   cupping her breasts   driving her
hips in a   v o l u p t u o u s   roll   *"Just two things
matter   --   sex   and death   Sex   is the fun part --
Death   --   not so much   What comes between?   Not my
department   Speak to the clerk in L – 5
or 6 "*   s/he said   waving a hand   and   winkled
effortless   into   a priapic   he
who pranced   prick-proud   then shifted back to   s/he
*"WE   are the force that drives the fuse   to flower
  WE   make the womb   that grows the soil   where seed
falls   What part do you not get ?"*   s/he growled
and shifted   seamless   into   dark death
riding homeward   astride four   bone bare beasts

On the Care and Feeding of the Gods

Ichor makes them different   When you have
ichor in your veins   you live forever   and so
because they cannot die   the gods arise
each day to   sunny skies   fair winds   and
the only chance of rain   or ruin   is if --
a trifle bored   --   they clap their hands   and lo
it happens   Each perfect day some early
acolyte arrives   pitches the old dead
flowers out   and shakes the cloth   A second --
draped in status   bowing   offers each god an apple
garlands lilies in their hair   so heady sweet
Thus do they pass their days   :   in a fragrant haze
a drawn out daze   Such is the unending
life of   a well-tended god   wholesomely fed

Landscape with a Coming Storm

Sometimes   the mood of the world's   made manifest
Today seems such a day   with this dark sky
looming   There's no   avoiding it   I think
sunk low   in my own brooding   gloom   It is a threat
deepening   toward Prussian   a bruised hue   that
leadens us   It will   wash over us   roll
us   drown us   --   this anger   this unholy storm
Ahead may be   for some   a white spire   rising   --
bright Hope   with a cross on top   :   an anchor /
mooring   /   sanctuary   /   home   But not for me
For now the maelstrom blooms   Now comes lightning
and the fierce descending   We have entered
the eye of the storm   dear god   in whom
I do not believe   We cannot see

Perhaps to Dream

No sound   nor fury   --   nebulae look like every
thing   mind cannot imagine   but must try to name   :
crab nebula   horsehead nebula   nebula
like dark towers climbing   :   eyes   butterflies   lace
shedding   tatters   threading out   into the vast
ness of cosmos   There are even nebulae
that look like   no   *thing*   so much as   rank upon
rank   of the pipes of   an immense celestial
organ   vibrating   and reverberating
down   all   the unending   long halls   of
universe   Songs of the stuff of stars   :   collapse
and coalescence   dying and birthing   gas
dust   plasma   ash   Of these we are made   each
of us   and will return   :   silent   incorporeal

Naming the Rose

In the beginning   one hand clasping flower
to chest   is met by   one hand reaching for
possession   accompanied by   foot stomp
while other hand pounds chest   (*unhhh!*)   That
first word ?   *Mine! -- flower mine now*!   Now   and force
lacking subtlety   To become   *named*   word
required   a reaching out   :   *here* --   *you take it* :
bright   transcendent   syllables   companioned
together   --   modulate and ordered   Thus
friend   grows from :   *let us share*   Yet   this sweet
smelling flower   and bud   and stem   named in
binomial nomenclature   Rosa
rugosa   offered to you   :   *here*   *pretty* --
remains by nature   *thumb- prick*   *blood-spiller*

LADY MANTIS PRAYS BEFORE LUNCH

Dear Lord   I am devout   about   devouring
Every day   I raise my arms   and pray   --   claws
clenched tight   --   please   send me   something bright
and beautiful   to bite   I am no different
than the stealing fox   or soaring kite   Send me
red twig gossamer   --   a dainty damselfly
in flight   I've heard   she   is a mighty huntress
too   --   though   I do not understand   her weapons
Dear Lord   how much   better   beautiful
tastes to bite   Just yesterday   as I clung
to a branch   one bright   bejeweled   hummingbird
flew by and   *snap !*   oh!   the joy   of the green
struggle !   --   we both prayed   --   I held him for a
  long   long   time   feeling the heat of his heart

The World Tree   Blasted

At bloom time   white blossoms   filled the air
with honey scent   and   tiny hummingbirds
shot   up   up   faster than arrows   --   straight or
sometimes   spiraling   to hover   perch lightly
there   high in the tree   of which   now   mere
blackened shaft is left   where once was curving
grace of line   crayoning   toward sky   anchoring
tree to earth   --   to underworld   Now one stark
branch   at awkward angle   blackly juts   If
in every storm   is a final   battle   then
every tree is living myth   and it was
right   that vulture   lofted   down   so low and
slow /   lurched to landing /   heavy /   brooding /   black
shouldered   /   blotting heaven   /   hunched

AFTER BUSON

I feel   reverberation   in my skull
the sound of the bell   *as it leaves the bell*
I feel   I hear   the thump of the towers
jumping on their grassed   ground scape   --   though this
happens   only in the small screen   of my
hand held phone   --   the image entirely
eye   There is no sound   thump   impact   or
reverberation   What   *feels*   is pure
body   tuned toward *answer*   :   Respond   --   we
cannot help it   our nerve fibers all so
exquisitely connected   aligned   so that
we feel   what we have not felt   hear   --   *coolness*
he   called it   --   sound   long after the silence
fell to internal echoes   :   the stilled bell

Barbed : Then and Now

'homo homini lupus est' : Plautus

It was Acanthus mollis   that found its soft
voluptuous   way   a-top the severe slim
columns   of the temple   of   Olympian Zeus
that took six hundred years to build   and was
finished   at last   only to endure intact a single
century   before being reduced to   a stockpile of
marble construction blocks   Those columns needed
spikes   :   A. spinosus   –   each lurid leaf and flower
armored   Walking past it several times each day
I think   surely a plant for a feral culture :
barbed   as in barbarian   What use sweet reason
when the wolves sweep down?   howling   Death !
Death !   (yours – not theirs)   destruction
singing   through their veins   their shining eyes

PRISMED

Captured in a crystal cage   light   faceted
turns in the window   Its nearest face
is tangible   /   flat   Its side facets   /   seen
a-slant /   distort   Through the glass   the far sides   –
seen   not darkly   but   as though through some
faint obscuring veil   --   can be surmised   Each next
facet   is   revealed   as   the   prism   turns
Each turn   turns one face true   for its own brief
time   All the facets fracture light   --   do light
violence   Truth/s fly off   and cast sharp shards
into the dim   Their colors cut   --   the walls within
bleed rainbows   Yet through the windows   light pours
in / shuddering rainbows / shedding truths   It shines
withal   and gleans and gathers   light abundant

CUSP

Nadir   zenith   cusp   are places   --   but cusp is
also passage   –   a place between   In the wood
locust and maple are   behind   the cusp   that
yesterday   were before it   and when all
the trees are bare   they will be   over the cusp
as in tomorrow   and tomorrow...   But today
the oaks are right   on   the cusp   in shades of rose
tan   and pale yellow   with tints of orange   and
the sun's warm   long   slanted   light   shines through
their glassine leaves   to shadow leaves   below
and glow   And so it was for my mother   in her
passing   --   her skin fragile   luminous   a chrysalis
lit from within   with the thing inside   tremulous
wondering   if its parents are still alive

Liminal

The Legend of the Night Cry birds

Soul Sucker   moth-owl   harbinger   you call us
We are the cryptic   whispers   in the day's
bright glades   --   our liminal nature   stirs   your
unease   When dusk   thresholds   into night   --   then
we fly   long winged   and low   That's when you
fear us   in those ambiguous hours   We see
them then   --   the lost souls   that loft into
the air   like   pale moths   In pity   we call :
Come!   Ride the night air!'   and gather them   --   in
to our secret nests   to keep them safe   one night
At dawn they   lift   and rise   and melt away
Whip poor-will   whip poor-will   Are we their last
remembrance   of the day bright glades?   We cannot
say   We cannot hold them   They cannot stay

ON THE DAY OF THE DEAD

My mother   will unpack herself   from her box of
ashes   move to a comfortable chair   look at me
critically   and say : You're wearing *that*?   And maybe
this time   I will have the   will to   not   run and change
my clothes   My father will re-assemble himself from
the soil under the lemon tree   in Arizona   come
north for the day   sit at the table drooped   scowling
over his cigarette   like a crow   or Ichibod Crane
while my brother   who brought him   mutters   :   *humph*
humph   at all he disapproves of   on principle
which is everything   --   my house   my head   my heart
Toward the end   my dead lover will come   line them up
dance them all back to dust   while I smile   and wave   --
crying   :   Goodbye!   Goodby again   Same time next year?

THE FLEDGLING

Look   here's God   sparkling in the trees   Rain
fell in the still-dark morning   leaving bright
drops   God-traces   caught and cupped   :   in each leaf
a God-mote   --   and look   here too is God's bright
face   wafting   lofting   in the delirious
perfumed air   and the bees rest in the phlox
so darkly sated   with God-drink   they cannot
move
              //

                    For days now we have been hearing
first here   then there   calling   each to each   a
hawk   and her child   a fledgling   full lost
in the pain   of its impending parting   --
crying   *find me*   *feed me*   *mother!*   Lying
here   with my knee pain   pained by the world's deep
need   and pain   I too cry   :   Find me!   --   *Seek...*

In the dark hours   I awake   :   some small beast
in terror   is fending off attack   In this
too   is the divine   --   that face we do not
like to face   Then   in day   back on my
porch   warmth dazed once more   I watch bemused
the hum   and happy-seeming-ness of life --
goldfinch on sunflower   robin hopping to
feed her own fledgling   standing in the street
with mouth agape   --   knowing that   above
somewhere   is a young hawk   learning to feed
itself   It took to the air   They are aloft
now   We see them   soaring   swooping --   low
shadows   swift across the earth

                                        //

                                                There is a
cold clean current   hidden   in the day's warm air

Some weeks have passed   --   my knee is healing
It's been a gift   to be obliged to   watch   /
wait   /   wonder   /   The hawk child is far ranging
now   flies wide   climbs high   --   it's voice a distant
pulse   --   language   passing through the air
sharing   information I can only
guess   --   how   perhaps   there is a vole   darting
from bush to hole   upon the earth below
What dangers   of rare devising   await
a hawk not yet wise to its world?   And that
other fledgling?
                    //
                         It rained again   The rain fell in
the still-dark morning   God-motes   --   bright drops
sparkling   caught   and cupped   within each
leaf   ... and the bees doze darkly   in the phlox

LITTLE GRIEFS

It was a small yellow parakeet   clutching
as for dear life   the window wiper of my car
that allowed one finger   to reach a hand's width
closer   before it flew away   landing on Starbuck's
awning   and joined there by a goldfinch   mad
with territoriality   or lust   (that brighter yellow)
hard to know which   My grandmother had a bird
she loved   that rode her shoulder   everywhere
until one day   forgetting   she stepped outside
It's the little griefs that break us   In the old
world she'd lost her siblings   to diphtheria   :
only she survived   Heavy   the burden
the cross of innocence   --   of all unintended
sacrifices   to the hawks of fate

A Prayer from the Prayer Adverse

How close despair   and prayer   lie down in bed
born of the same love   and   through the same eyes
see both fore and aft   :   that squirrel offers sun
flowers to feathered gods   :   that locust sheds tears
as leaves   :   how mute swan swims   in now murky
meres   and the strangled oak dies   gleaned   Through
the same eyes   --   those hidden eyes   --   they see
Wither the wild crane   and whippoorwill?   --   seals
sadness to silence   and tightens the throat
Despair   inarticulate   ends   all   :   Yet
through those eyes   those hidden eyes   there may
still come a lightening   :   a prayer -- un-glossed --
if an un-glossed prayer may hope   For all
that I love   some slight brightening

NOTCHING THE WHEEL

There goes another   notch   on the wheel   :   goldfinch
changing his summer garb   to drab sparrow guise –
the way   the missus goes   all year   only a hint
of yellow   leaking through   as he barbers sunflowers
And now comes actea round again   --   she of many
names / cohosh / bugbane / cimicifuga   :   *Fairy
candles*   that open their small white asterisks
and   cast out their honey-scent   to draw in late
bumbling bees   The trees are breaking their too --
green – too -- chemical bonds   Origami is at
her drawing board   in the attic   lost in dreams of
color : crimson   vermillion   coral lake   In
the wings   Dragon   quietly   fans his icy
breath   listening   for the next notch of the wheel

THE AGING GARDENER LAMENTS SEPTEMBER

Lord   Lord   What a mess the garden is   --   not
a modicum of order   here   and me   supposed
to set a good example   I've hacked back that
promiscuous bitch   'Pamina'   --   all her skirt
foliage   I've ripped away   and some of her
children   too   (murderer!)   I've beaten into
submission   the overly exuberant   'Rozanne'
(back   back! you beast!)   Goldfinch lay waste
the ripe sunflowers   A dozen different insects
are pillaging   sedum   agastache   and anything
else   that dares   remain in bloom   A few beans still
hang from   utterly   leafless plants   like limp tinsel   or
draped dregs   from a party   that's gone on too long   –
none of us   staggering home   in good shape

THANKSGIVING BRIAR

Down   at the   edge   of the house foundation
briar grows   --   paid no mind all year   except
as weed   absently noted   a plant that prickled
touch   allowed life   largely for its   --   and my   --
lack of ambition   Where another plant
might strive to conquer   briar deferred   and thus
survived   three shoots only   lying almost
parallel to ground   --   studies   at this time
of year in   *there-is-no-name-for-this-color*   :
here raspberry   or   maroon   no   --   mahogany
blushed with *bloom*   Colors   glaucous as fog   :   lilac
laid over violet   lavender   sky-blue   --   In
the moment of naming   to find the color
that had hidden   in the space   *between*   --   slid   on

Song : Storm after Drought

This time   the deluge came   and went   quickly
washing the day's heat away   after night
had fallen   silent   to the hot pavement
There is   no more racing   the night track   in
blackness   bringing the horses safely home
-- that little lie   allowing me   to bolt   --   like my
beasts   fully alive to the flashing skies
Today   is three weeks out from solstice   They're
long dead   all those beautiful horses   and
I've grown old   Last night's rain   tapered down from
un - gentleness   to less than a deluge   soft --
soaking the parched skins of earth   Underneath
the streetlamps   small   wet   leaves   sparkle   Almost
imperceptibly   the long summer days   wane

BUGBANE

One single plant blooms   this November   among
the ruins of   my small front yard garden   amid
limp sunflowers   hanging a-droop stalks   so spent
even the hungry goldfinch   has deserted   But
blooms of actea   --   bugbane   --   stand tall   --   taller
than sunflowers   stiff   up right   braced against
cold destruction   Their long up-reaching stalks
(color of aubergine)   explode   from ferned
foliage below   and now prolong their final riot
The buds   --   black pearls   lined up on plum spikes
open unordered   one   bud   at   a   time   Star
burst filaments   flare   like white asterisks   burn
down black lines   where   one late bee roots in
honey-scented rockets   that scour cold air

THE ROCK

Do you see   those two children   --   she behind
frowning   stumbling to keep up   --   he in front
bouncing   buoyed like air   a smile - bright light
shining   his small brown face   Do you   also
remember   how it feels   before a storm
when the charged air picks up ?   When you were
a child   did that fierce storm   energy never
take you   so you bucked   and galloped   in
the living air   --   until the storm broke   and clean
rain pounded down ?   Sometimes it seems   one
child dances   along all his paths   --   even
in storms   --   while another lags   like a dead
weight   drags her down   Heart heavy   --   dearly
burdened   she cannot skip before the storm

Redux   The Care and Feeding of the Gods

But never   let a god taste blood   nor touch   one
drop   for blood and ichor   mixed   change to
elixir   which goes   straight to their heads   burns
there wonderfully   buzzes   Air   becomes a
golden glow   that tastes in their bellowed lungs
like honey   tongued   and a small lust starts   for
sacrifice   :   cricket   mouse   a little bird
A strong god   can resist for years   that growing
need   but in the end   ah!   for a dozen
maidens   danced to death   in the springtime
or   one hundred heads   held up by dripping
hands   and   in the end   an oven   or a blast
that can burn ten million souls   in one glorious
burst   *Violence*   :   this is the nectar of the gods

Un - time

Is the   pause   before the action has   lost
hope of a   miracle   Reverse !   (re / verse !)
Un - time   is the time   between   the bite thought
of   and the bite   taken   *with the bright of*
it   tasting   upon the lips   It is what
happens   in an eye-blink   when the lids close
then   unnoticed   open wide again   or
don't   --   between the end of one wor(l)d   and
the start of another   --   between the end of
one life   and the start of   what comes after
or   does not   Between hope and hope   or hope
and despair   as when a swimmer has seen
his savior   lift   from his throne   but not yet
leave it   as the swimmer sinks

Window Between Worlds

Hearts beat   --   the cats and   the hearts of sparrows
in the barberry bush   full of red berries
and small brown birds   eyeing   the cats that lie
with feet   tucked   tension in bodies   fur fluffed like
the sparrow's feathers   inches away   out -
side two panes of   thermal sealed glass   except
sparrows are fluffed for weather   not lust for
blood   The birds hold still   as the snow drifts down
They're used to cats   --   but not to me   When I
look through the glass that lets birds look   in   while
cats look   out   they flock   up   from sanctuary
triggering   flinch   in cats / ears flicked flat   In seconds
truce returns   All settle   Nothing -- really --
has changed   But in the hush   hearts   beat faster

THE UNLOOKED FOR GIFT

Is this the hawk   I saw in that bare tree   months ago
staring down with savage eyes?   Look at her   lying
cold   under this bush   that is   barely left to life
She looks as though she   huddled   to hide from death
before death found   her   that found death for   so many
other small creatures   or   perhaps death caught her
unawares   in flight   and left her here   lying with head
sprawled   taloned feet   curled   as if struck from above
while carrying small squirrel   or chipmunk   prised
claws limp   suddenly   and useless   She   that
embodied predatory grace   fell   graceless
Closely seen   how beautiful   fanned on bare earth
these checkered wings   that powered
drive   and dive   and flight

A Poem to Comfort Robin

Perhaps she is   even now running   happy
on that vast beach beside the wide lapping
infinity sea   The cease-less waves roll
white capped   onto the broad sloping gentle
shore   Gulls congregate in bunches   Sand
pipers run   in   and   out   of shallow water
Sun shines   while the air is cool   She has been
filled with love   your little dog   She wants for
nothing   Her coat is white and fluffy   There
are no longer lumps to pain her   --   her breath
comes easy   --   she is healed   That is enough
until the day   far distant   which will seem a
moment to her   when she finds   footprints in the sands
she knows   :   Joy will come to her   then   with a leap

Omens

She is naked again   --   Honey Locust
has shed her golden skin   sure sign of the advent
of fall   Portents :   our eyes look out   and see
while the white core   at the heart of the brain
selects   connects   makes meanings   /   some true
some false   some fantastic   Sometimes we see
without seeing   hear   without hearing   --   or
see more   hear more   than is there   Beloved
what shall we do?   The wind speaks in whispers
meanings we cannot discern   Is it an
omen   --   that single cloud   in the west with
the golden lining?   Or there   to the north
over the lake   where the whole wide sky   fills
with a dark   descending   What should we believe?

ABOUT THE AUTHOR

ELSA JOHNSON has spent most of her life living among and appreciating the green verdant hills and valleys, ledges, streams and bogs of northeastern Ohio (last of the Appalachian foothills—a place that unequivocally wants to be a forest). She is a poet, writer, landscape designer, artist, and hands-on environmental sustainability advocate, invasive species warrior, and a passionate volunteer in nearby Forest Hill Park. She lives in Cleveland Heights.